Jesus Grows Up

Jesus Grows Up

Text and illustrations: Pilar Paris, Josep M. Lozano and Maria Rius

English adaptation: Caryl Green

Cover design: Gilles Lépine

This book was published originally in 1995
by Editorial Claret, S.A., in Barcelona, Spain, entitled, *Hablemos de Jesús*.

English version, Copyright © 1997 Novalis
49 Front St. E., 2nd Floor, Toronto, Ontario M5E 1B3 Canada

Canadian Cataloguing in Publication Data

Paris, Pilar
  Jesus Grows Up

Originally published 1995 in Spanish under title:
  Hablemos de Jesús. Also published 1996 in French
  under title: Parlons de Jésus.

ISBN 2-89088-895-9

  1. Jesus Christ–Childhood–Juvenile literature.
I. Lozano, Josep Maria, 1954- II. Rius, Maria III. Title.

BT302.P37 1997   j232.92   C97-900581-7

Published in the United States by St. Anthony Messenger Press,
1615 Republic St., Cincinnati, OH 45210-1298
ISBN 0-86716-331-3

Printed and bound in Spain

Jesus Grows Up

Pilar Paris • Josep M. Lozano • Maria Rius

ST. ANTHONY MESSENGER PRESS
Cincinnati, Ohio

NOVALIS

A long time ago, God sent the angel Gabriel to the town of Nazareth
to visit a young girl named Mary, who was engaged to Joseph, a carpenter.
The angel said to her: "Hello, Mary! God is with you!"

Mary wondered what this greeting could mean. But the angel went on:
"Do not be afraid. God loves you very much. You will be a mother soon:
you will have a baby and you will call him Jesus."

"How can this be," Mary asked the angel, "for I have no husband?"
The angel answered her: "The Holy Spirit will take care of everything
for this child will come from God. He will be holy and will be called the Son of God."

"Your cousin, Elizabeth, also is expecting a baby, even though she is old.
You see, nothing is impossible for God!" Then Mary said: "I am the servant of the Lord.
Let everything happen as you have said!" And the angel left her.

A little while later, Mary decided to visit her cousin Elizabeth
who lived far away in a village in the mountains.

When she arrived at the house where Elizabeth and her husband Zechariah lived,
Mary greeted her cousin.

Immediately Elizabeth felt her baby move inside her and she exclaimed:
"You are the most blessed of all women and blessed is the fruit of your womb!"
Mary replied with a prayer:

"My soul gives glory to the Lord, and I am filled with joy when I think of God, my Saviour, because he has looked upon his little servant. And people will call me blessed forever because the all-powerful God has done great things for me!"

Mary stayed with Elizabeth for three months and then returned home.
Soon she and Joseph were married.

As for Elizabeth, she gave birth to a little boy who was named John.

At that time, the emperor Caesar Augustus declared
that a census of the whole empire was to take place
and all people had to be registered in the town where they were born.

That is why Joseph and Mary went to Bethlehem.
It was almost time for Mary to have her baby. Bethlehem was very crowded…
Joseph and Mary had nowhere to spend the night.

15

Because there was no room for them at the inn,

they settled down in the cave where the animals were kept,

and that is where the baby was born.

Mary wrapped him in some cloths and put him in a manger to sleep.

Not far away, some shepherds were spending the night in the fields,
guarding their sheep. Suddenly, one of God's angels
appeared to them in a dazzling light, and they were very frightened.

"Do not be afraid," said the angel. "I have good news for you: today, in Bethlehem, a Saviour has been born for you! This is how you will know him: you will find a newborn baby wrapped in cloths and lying in a manger."

"Let's go to Bethlehem!" the shepherds said.
They hurried off and found Mary, Joseph and the baby in a stable,
just as the angel had said.

Having worshipped the newborn baby, the shepherds returned to their flocks,
filled with wonder at what had happened that night.
They told everyone they met all about it.

Soon the time came to name the baby.
This was the celebration of circumcision,

and he was given the name Jesus:
the name the angel had told Mary to give him.

A few weeks later, Joseph and Mary brought Jesus to the Temple in Jerusalem
to present him to God and to give thanks.
They thanked God by offering two doves.

An old man named Simeon – a wise and fair man – lived in Jerusalem.
The Holy Spirit had told him that he would not die
before seeing the Saviour promised by the prophets.

Taking the baby Jesus in his arms, Simeon blessed God saying:
"Lord, now I can die for I have seen the Saviour you promised us."

Joseph and Mary were amazed to hear these words.

At the same time, a very old woman named Anna arrived.
Anna served God in the Temple.

She, too, thanked God for this little child,
and said he was the Saviour of the world.

When they had finished all the things they had to do in Jerusalem,

Joseph and Mary returned home with the child to Nazareth in Galilee.

At this time, living in the East, were some very learned people
who studied the sky and the stars. They were called Magi.

One night they saw a star appear – a star bigger and brighter than all the others…
They knew that the star foretold a special happening in Judea…
the birth of a king who would be the Messiah, the Saviour.

They set off to follow the star. When they arrived in Jerusalem they asked:
"Where is the king who was just born?
We saw his star and have come to honour him."

When King Herod heard this news he was shocked…
A new king!
The whole town was talking about it.

He called the high priests and the teachers of the Law
and asked them where the Messiah was to be born.
They answered him:

"In Bethlehem in Judea; that is what is written."
Then Herod called the Magi and sent them to Bethlehem, saying:

"Go and see what is happening and, when you have found the child,
let me know so that I too may go and honour him."

With these instructions from the king, the Magi continued their journey,
happy that the star they had seen in the East
once again showed them the way.

Finally the star stopped over a house.
They went into the house and found the child with his mother, Mary,
and they knelt and worshipped him.

Then they offered him precious gifts: gold, incense and myrrh.
But they were warned in a dream not to go back to Herod,
so they returned to their home country by another way.

Jesus grew up with Mary and Joseph.
In the evening, when Joseph lit the lamp, Jesus noticed that the lamp wasn't hidden,
but rather was placed up high so it could light the entire room.

And Jesus often watched his mother kneading bread,
and he could see the yeast she put with the flour
made the dough rise to make good bread.

He watched the shepherds looking after their sheep all around Nazareth.
He saw that a good shepherd knows all his sheep
and that the sheep know their shepherd.

He also learned that a shepherd who has one hundred sheep,
if he loses one, will leave the others on their own
to go search for the one that is lost and bring it back.

He wanted everyone to be happy,
from the richest to the poorest person,
and to share in God's feast.

He would have liked to tell each person he met on the road:
"You too are invited!"

At harvest time, when Jesus played marbles with the village children,
he often saw grains of wheat roll on the road, fall on the stones or disappear in the weeds;
but others fell in the good soil.

He saw how even the smallest of all the seeds grows until its branches become so big that the birds can fly to its shade to shelter themselves from the sun.

Jesus was learning what life was all about.

He was growing in strength and wisdom before God
and those who knew him.

Every year his parents went to Jerusalem for the Festival of Passover.

When Jesus was twelve years old, he went with them to Jerusalem.

When the festival was over,
Joseph and Mary started on their journey home,

but Jesus stayed in Jerusalem without telling them...

Thinking he was walking with his friends, Mary and Joseph were not worried.
However, after not seeing him for the entire day,
they looked for him among their relatives and friends…

Jesus was nowhere to be found!
What now?
They walked all the way back to Jerusalem.

59

Finally, on the third day of searching, they found him!
Jesus was in the Temple, sitting among the teachers and the learned ones,

listening to them and asking them a thousand questions…
All who heard him were amazed at his understanding and the wisdom of his answers.

His mother said to him: "My son, why did you do this to us? Your father and I have been very worried and we looked everywhere for you!" "Why were you looking for me?" replied Jesus. "Do you not know that I must be with my Father?"

He was speaking of God, but Mary and Joseph did not understand what he meant.
Jesus returned with them to Nazareth and he continued to love and obey them.